WHY ARE ELECTIONS IMPORTANT?

By Jacqueline Laks Gorman
Reading consultant: Susan Nations, M.Ed.,
author/literacy coach/consultant in literacy development

WEEKLY READER®

PUBLISHING

Please visit our web site at www.garethstevens.com
For a free color catalog describing our list of high-quality books,
call 1-800-542-2595 (USA) or 1-800-387-3178 (Canada). Our fax: 1-877-542-2596

Library of Congress Cataloging-in-Publication Data

Gorman, Jacqueline Laks, 1955-
    Why are elections important? / Jacqueline Laks Gorman.
       p. cm. — (Know your government)
    Includes index.
    ISBN-13: 978-0-8368-8842-3 (lib. bdg.)
    ISBN-10: 0-8368-8842-1 (lib. bdg.)
    ISBN-13: 978-0-8368-8847-8 (softcover)
    ISBN-10: 0-8368-8847-2 (softcover)
    1. Elections—United States—Juvenile literature.
  2. Voting—United States—Juvenile literature. I. Title.
  JK1978.G67   2008
  324.973—dc22   2007035504

This edition first published in 2008 by
Weekly Reader® Books
An Imprint of Gareth Stevens Publishing
1 Reader's Digest Road
Pleasantville, NY 10570-7000 USA

Copyright © 2008 by Gareth Stevens, Inc.

Senior Editor: Brian Fitzgerald
Creative Director: Lisa Donovan
Senior Designer: Keith Plechaty
Layout: Cynthia Malaran
Photo Research: Charlene Pinckney and Kimberly Babbitt

Photo credits: cover & title page © Tom Grill/Corbis; p. 5 The Granger Collection; p. 7 Frank Wiese/AP;
p. 8 Mark Humphrey/AP; pp. 10, 11, 13 © Bettmann/Corbis; p. 14 Courtesy Office of the Governor, State
of Alaska; p. 15 Chip East/Reuters/Corbis; p. 16 Margo Cohn Pactanac/AP; p. 18 Randy Snyder/AP;
p. 19 Courtesy Ronald Reagan Presidential Library; p. 20 Joe Raedle/Getty Images; p. 21 © Steven
Clevenger/Corbis

Printed in the United States of America

1 2 3 4 5 6 7 8 9 10 09 08 07

TABLE OF CONTENTS

Words that appear in the glossary are printed in **boldface** type the first time they appear in the text.

CHAPTER 1

Government by the People

In the 1700s, the country of Great Britain ruled America. Americans could not **elect,** or choose, their own leaders. The people did not have any say in making laws. Americans decided to fight a war for their freedom. They defeated the British army and formed the United States.

The leaders of the United States formed a **democracy.** A democracy is a government that is run by the people. People hold **elections** to choose their leaders. They also vote on issues that are important to them. Voting gives people a say in how the country is run.

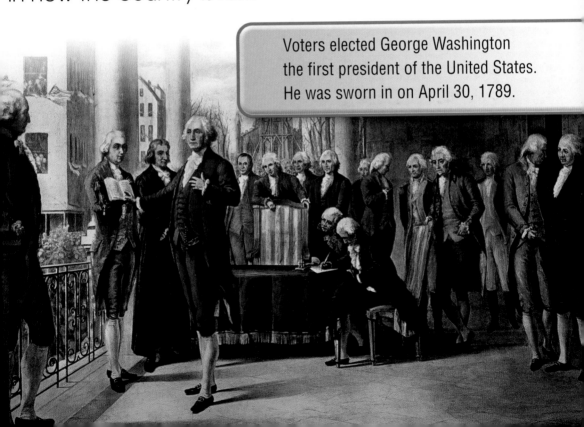

Voters elected George Washington the first president of the United States. He was sworn in on April 30, 1789.

CHAPTER 2

An Important Right

You may belong to a club or group at school. To get things done, you and the other members of the group need to work together. The group decides together on rules and chooses its leaders. Often you make these decisions by voting. Voting is a way for a group to make decisions.

Voters sometimes wait in long lines to vote on Election Day.

Voting is one of the most important rights that Americans have. By voting, Americans take part in their government. They show that they care about their community. Voting gives people a voice in how their town, state, and country are run.

Before Election Day, voters see a lot of signs for the people running for office.

Americans vote for leaders they think will do the best job. They also vote on issues that are important to their state or town. Voters may decide when to build new roads or schools.

CHAPTER 3

Who Can Vote?

When the United States was formed, many people were not allowed to vote. Almost all voters were white men who owned land. Women, Native Americans, and most African Americans could not vote. People who did not own land did not have the right to vote.

Over the years, new laws were passed that allowed more people to vote. In 1870, all African American men gained the right to vote. In 1920, all women gained the right, too. Four years later, Native Americans also gained the right to vote.

All African American men were allowed to vote for the first time in the late 1800s.

Teens voted for president for the first time during the 1972 election.

Until 1971, a voter had to be at least twenty-one years old. Today, almost any U.S. **citizen** who is at least eighteen years old can vote. In most states, people have to register, or sign up, to vote.

PRIMARY BALLOT

REPUBLICAN PRIMARY BALLOT

CHAPTER 4

What Leaders Do We Elect?

Voters elect leaders for their country, state, and town. All voters in the United States can vote for the president and vice president. The president and vice president run as a team. They work in Washington, D.C. Voters elect other leaders who work there, too.

Voters choose the people who represent them in Congress. Congress is the part of government that makes laws. The two parts of Congress are the Senate and the House of Representatives.

There are 100 **senators.** Each of the fifty states elects two senators. There are 435 members of the House of Representatives. States that have more people elect more **representatives.**

In 1968, Shirley Chisholm from New York became the first African American woman elected to Congress.

Alaska Governor Sarah Palin visited with students in the city of Fairbanks. She is the first female governor of Alaska.

The people in each state elect a **governor.** The governor is the leader of the state government. The voters in each state also vote for members of the state **legislature.** The people in the legislature make state laws.

Most states are divided into smaller areas called **counties.** The voters in each county elect leaders who do important county jobs.

Voters in many towns and cities elect a **mayor.** Voters also elect the city or town **council.** The council makes laws for the city or town.

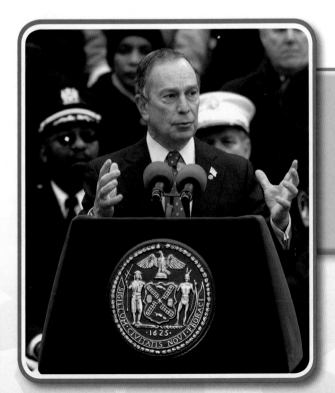

The voters in New York City elected Michael Bloomberg mayor in 2001. He was elected again in 2005.

Judges are in charge of courts. The president chooses the judges for the Supreme Court. The Supreme Court is the most important court in the country. The president chooses other top judges, too. In most states, voters elect judges who run state and town courts.

A state judge (left) is sworn in after winning an election. Judges promise to treat people fairly in court.

CHAPTER 5

When Are Elections Held?

Election Day is often the first Tuesday in November. In years that end in an even number (such as 2008 and 2010), voters choose leaders for the whole country. Voters elect a president and vice president every four years. Senators have to run for election every six years. Members of the House of Representatives run every two years.

People running in local elections often go door-to-door to meet voters at their homes.

People also vote for state and town leaders on Election Day. In most states, voters elect a governor every four years. Other state and local leaders are elected in different years in different states. People may also vote on important issues in their state or local community.

Before they vote, people learn about the **candidates.** These are people who run for office. People read about the candidates and watch them on TV. Voters pick candidates who feel the same as they do on important issues.

More than 65 million people watched a debate on television between President Ronald Reagan (right) and Walter Mondale in 1984.

People use special machines to vote on Election Day. Everyone's vote is kept secret.

On Election Day, voters go to schools, churches, and other places in their town to vote. All of the candidates are listed on a **ballot.** Voters pick the candidates they like best.

At the end of the day, all the votes are counted. Then the winners are named.

Voting gives people a chance to make a difference in their community.

Voting is important, but not everyone chooses to vote. Only about six out of ten people vote in the election for president. Even fewer people vote in local elections. Everyone should vote so he or she has a voice in how the country is run. Every vote is important. Every vote counts!

Glossary

ballot: a list of the people running in an election

candidate: a person who is running for office

citizen: an official member of a country who has certain rights, such as voting

council: a group of people who are elected to make decisions for a city or town

county: a part of a state that has its own local government

democracy: a system of government in which people vote for their leaders

elect: to choose a leader by voting

election: a time when citizens vote for their leaders

governor: the head of a state government

legislature: the part of a government that makes the laws

mayor: the head of a city or town government

representative: a member of the House of Representatives, one of the two parts of Congress

senator: a member of the Senate, one of the two parts of Congress

To Find Out More

Books

Voting. A True Book (series). Sarah De Capua (Children's Press)

Voting and Elections. Let's See Library: Our Nation (series).
Patricia J. Murphy (Compass Point Books)

What Are Elections? First Guide to Government (series).
Nancy Harris (Heinemann)

Web Sites
Election Process
bensguide.gpo.gov/3-5/election/index.html
This site explains how national leaders are elected.

Inside the Voting Booth
pbskids.org/democracy/vote
This site lets you find out what it's like to vote and why voting is
so important.

Publisher's note to educators and parents: Our editors have carefully reviewed
these web sites to ensure that they are suitable for children. Many web sites
change frequently, however, and we cannot guarantee that a site's future
contents will continue to meet our high standards of quality and educational
value. Be advised that children should be closely supervised whenever they
access the Internet.

Index

About the Author

Jacqueline Laks Gorman grew up in New York City. She attended Barnard College and Columbia University, where she received a master's degree in American history. She has worked on many kinds of books and has written several series for children and young adults. She now lives in DeKalb, Illinois, with her husband, David, and children, Colin and Caitlin. She registered to vote when she turned eighteen and votes in every election.